God's Promises For Women

Compiled by Larry Richards

To: _____

As you read these verses and meditate on them, you will find them
a source of guidance, for God points us in his Word to a productive and
meaningful life. You will also find them a source of strength, for
here too are God's promises, reassuring you that the Lord is committed
to help you become the Christian woman you yearn to be.

From: _____

God's Promises for Women
Copyright © 1993 by The Zondervan Corporation

ISBN: 0-310-96203-X

Excerpts taken from:
The Christian Woman's Promise Book
Copyright © 1994 by The Zondervan Corporation

Scripture taken from the HOLY BIBLE: NEW INTERNATIONAL VERSION® (North American Edition). Copyright © 1973, 1978, 1984, by International Bible Society. Used by permission of Zondervan Publishing House. All rights reserved.

"NIV" and "New International Version" trademarks are registered in the United States Patent and Trademark Office by International Bible Society.

All rights reserved. No part of this publication may be reproduced, stored in a retrieval system, or transmitted in any form or by any means—electronic, mechanical, photocopy, recording, or any other—except for brief quotations in printed reviews, without the prior permission of the publisher.

Request for information should be addressed to:

ZondervanPublishingHouse
Grand Rapids, Michigan 49530

Project Editor: Jennifer Schnur

Printed in China

97 98 /HK/ 7 6

January 1

My Identity As a Christian Woman

I Am Created in God's Image

God created man in his own image, in the image of God he created him; male and female he created them. God blessed them and said to them, "Be fruitful and increase in number; fill the earth and subdue it."

Genesis 1:27–28

New Year's Day

My Inner Life As a Christian Woman
How I Deal With Self-Doubt

May our Lord Jesus Christ himself and God our Father, who loved us and by his grace gave us eternal encouragement and good hope, encourage your hearts and strengthen you in every good deed and word.

2 Thessalonians 2:16–17

New Year's Eve

My Identity As a Christian Woman
I Am Saved by Christ's Sacrifice

But because of his great love for us, God, who is rich in mercy, made us alive with Christ even when we were dead in transgressions—it is by grace you have been saved.

Ephesians 2:4–5

My Inner Life As a Christian Woman
How I Develop a Prayer Life

In my distress I called to the LORD; I cried to my God for help. From his temple he heard my voice; my cry came before him, into his ears.

Psalm 18:6

My Identity As a Christian Woman
I Am Part of God's Family

The Spirit himself testifies with our spirit that we are God's children. Now if we are children, then we are heirs—heirs of God and co-heirs with Christ.

Romans 8:16–17

My Inner Life As a Christian Woman
How I Get the Most From Scripture

*J*esus said, "If you hold to my teaching, you are really my disciples. Then you will know the truth, and the truth will set you free."

John 8:31–32

My Identity As a Christian Woman

I Am Indwelt by God's Spirit

I will give you a new heart and put a new spirit in you; I will remove from you your heart of stone and give you a heart of flesh. And I will put my Spirit in you and move you to follow my decrees and be careful to keep my laws.

Ezekiel 36:26–27

My Inner Life As a Christian Woman
How I Deal With Anxiety and Worry

Even though I walk through the valley of the shadow of death, I will fear no evil, for you are with me; your rod and your staff, they comfort me.

Psalm 23:4

January 5

My Identity As a Christian Woman
I Am Gifted to Serve Others

There are different kinds of gifts, but the same Spirit. There are different kinds of service, but the same Lord. There are different kinds of working, but the same God works all of them in all men. Now to each one the manifestation of the Spirit is given for the common good.
1 Corinthians 12:4–7

December 27

My Inner Life As a Christian Woman
How I Channel My Thought Life

The word of God is living and active. Sharper than any double-edged sword, it penetrates even to dividing soul and spirit, joints and marrow; it judges the thoughts and attitudes of the heart. Nothing in all creation is hidden from God's sight. Everything is uncovered and laid bare before the eyes of him to whom we must give account.

Hebrews 4:12–13

January 6

My Relationships As a Christian Woman
God's Ideal for My Marriage

The LORD God said, "It is not good for the man to be alone. I will make a helper suitable for him . . . the LORD God made a woman from the rib he had taken out of the man, and he brought her to the man. The man said, "This is now bone of my bones and flesh of my flesh; she shall be called 'woman,' for she was taken out of man." For this reason a man will leave his father and mother and be united to his wife, and they will become one flesh.

Genesis 2:18,22–24

My Relationships As a Christian Woman

How to Enrich My Relationships

He who covers over an offense promotes love, but whoever repeats the matter separates close friends.

Proverbs 17:9

January 7

My Relationships As a Christian Woman

My Role as a Wife

The husband should fulfill his marital duty to his wife, and likewise the wife to her husband. The wife's body does not belong to her alone but also to her husband. Do not deprive each other except by mutual consent and for a time, so that you may devote yourselves to prayer.

1 Corinthians 7:3–5

December 25

My Relationships As a Christian Woman
How to Enrich My Relationships

Do not lie to each other, since you have taken off your old self with its practices and put on the new self, which is being renewed . . . in the image of its Creator.

Colossians 3:9–10

Christmas Day

My Relationships As a Christian Woman
My Attitude Toward Sex

A man will leave his father and mother and be united to his wife, and they will become one flesh.

Genesis 2:24

My Relationships As a Christian Woman
My Fellowship With Others

Finally, all of you, live in harmony with one another; be sympathetic, love as brothers, be compassionate and humble.

1 Peter 3:8

Christmas Eve

My Relationships As a Christian Woman
My Approach to Conflict

And the Lord's servant must not quarrel; instead, he must be kind to everyone, able to teach, not resentful. Those who oppose him he must gently instruct.

2 Timothy 2:24–25

My Relationships As a Christian Woman
My Role in the Body of Christ

Lift up holy hands in prayer, without anger or disputing.

1 Timothy 2:8

My Relationships As a Christian Woman

My Approach to Hurt

Do not repay evil with evil or insult with insult, but with blessing, because to this you were called so that you may inherit a blessing.

1 Peter 3:9

My Relationships As a Christian Woman
How to Recognize a Good Church

Religion that God our Father accepts as pure and faultless is this: to look after orphans and widows in their distress and to keep oneself from being polluted by the world.

James 1:27

My Relationships As a Christian Woman
My Approach to Anger

*R*eckless words pierce like a sword, but the tongue of the wise brings healing.
Proverbs 12:18

My Relationships As a Christian Woman
How to Guide in Problem Situations

$\mathcal{D}$o not be misled: "Bad company corrupts good character."

1 Corinthians 15:33

My Relationships As a Christian Woman
My Approach to Weakness

The LORD *longs to be gracious to you; he rises to show you compassion.*
Isaiah 30:18

December 20

My Relationships As a Christian Woman
How to Guide in Problem Situations

Each one should test his own actions. Then he can take pride in himself, without comparing himself to somebody else.

Galatians 6:4

January 13

My Relationships As a Christian Woman
My Attitude Toward Openness

Speaking the truth in love, we will in all things grow up into him who is the Head, that is, Christ. From him the whole body, joined and held together by every supporting ligament, grows and builds itself up in love, as each part does its work.

Ephesians 4:15–16

December 19

My Relationships As a Christian Woman

How to Communicate Love

The Lord disciplines those he loves, and he punishes everyone he accepts as a son.
Hebrews 12:6

January 14

My Relationships As a Christian Woman
My Attitude Toward Forgiveness

If your brother sins, rebuke him, and if he repents, forgive him. If he sins against you seven times in a day, and seven times comes back to you and says, "I repent," forgive him.
Luke 17:3–4

December 18

My Relationships As a Christian Woman
My Resources for Discipline

God was reconciling the world to himself in Christ, not counting men's sins against them. And he has committed to us the ministry of reconciliation.

2 Corinthians 5:19

January 15

My Relationships As a Christian Woman
How to Mother

Keep his decrees and commands, which I am giving you today, so that it may go well with you and your children after you and that you may live long in the land the LORD your God gives you.

Deuteronomy 4:40

December 17

My Relationships As a Christian Woman
My Purpose in Discipline

Discipline your son, for in that there is hope; do not be a willing party to his death.
Proverbs 19:18

January 16

My Relationships As a Christian Woman
My Goals in Child Rearing

We dealt with each one of you as a father deals with his own children, encouraging, comforting and urging you to live lives worthy of God, who calls you into his kingdom and glory.

1 Thessalonians 2:11–12

December 16

My Relationships As a Christian Woman
My Attitude Toward Forgiveness

Bear with each other and forgive whatever grievances you may have against one another. Forgive as the Lord forgave you. And over all these virtues put on love, which binds them together in perfect unity.

Colossians 3:13

My Relationships As a Christian Woman
My Purpose in Discipline

God disciplines us for our good, that we may share in his holiness. No discipline seems pleasant at the time, but painful. Later on, however, it produces a harvest of righteousness and peace for those who have been trained by it.

Hebrews 12:10–11

My Relationships As a Christian Woman
My Attitude Toward Openness

We have spoken freely to you, Corinthians, and opened wide our hearts to you . . . open wide your hearts also.

2 Corinthians 6:11–13

My Relationships As a Christian Woman
My Resources for Discipline

Correct, rebuke and encourage—with great patience and careful instruction.
2 Timothy 4:2

My Relationships As a Christian Woman
My Approach to Weakness

Therefore, as God's chosen people, holy and dearly loved, clothe yourselves with compassion, kindness, humility, gentleness and patience.

Colossians 3:12

My Relationships As a Christian Woman
How to Encourage Spiritual Growth

He who seeks good finds goodwill, but evil comes to him who searches for it.
Proverbs 11:27

December 13

My Relationships As a Christian Woman
My Approach to Anger

In that day you will say: "I will praise you, O LORD. Although you were angry with me, your anger has turned away and you have comforted me."

Isaiah 12:1

My Relationships As a Christian Woman

How to Pray for My Children

I have not stopped giving thanks for you, remembering you in my prayers. I keep asking that the God of our Lord Jesus Christ, the glorious Father, may give you the Spirit of wisdom and revelation, so that you may know him better.

Ephesians 1:16–17

December 12

My Relationships As a Christian Woman

My Approach to Hurt

Commit your way to the LORD; trust in him and he will do this: He will make your righteousness shine like the dawn, the justice of your cause like the noonday sun.

Psalm 37:5–6

January 21

My Relationships As a Christian Woman

How to Communicate Love

This is how God showed his love among us: He sent his one and only Son into the world that we might live through him. This is love: not that we loved God, but that he loved us and sent his Son.

1 John 4:9–10

December 11

My Relationships As a Christian Woman
My Approach to Conflict

What causes fights and quarrels among you? Don't they come from your desires that battle within you? You want something but don't get it. You kill and covet, but you cannot have what you want. You quarrel and fight. You do not have, because you do not ask God.

James 4:1–2

January 22

My Relationships As a Christian Woman
How to Tell My Child About God

Tell your children and grandchildren how I dealt harshly with the Egyptians and how I performed my signs among them . . . that you may know that I am the LORD.

Exodus 10:2

My Relationships As a Christian Woman
My Attitude Toward Sex

So God created man in his own image, in the image of God he created him; male and female he created them.

Genesis 1:27

January 23

My Relationships As a Christian Woman
How to Guide in Problem Situations

Hatred stirs up dissension, but love covers over all wrongs.

Proverbs 10:12

December 9

My Relationships As a Christian Woman
My Attitude Toward Money

Command those who are rich in this present world not to be arrogant nor to put their hope in wealth, which is so uncertain, but to put their hope in God, who richly provides us with everything for our enjoyment. Command them to do good, to be rich in good deeds, and to be generous and willing to share.

1 Timothy 6:17–18

My Relationships As a Christian Woman
How to Guide in Problem Situations

Do not accuse a man for no reason—when he has done you no harm.
Proverbs 3:30

December 8

My Relationships As a Christian Woman
How to Introduce a Person to Jesus

Always be prepared to give an answer to everyone who asks you to give the reason for the hope that you have. But do this with gentleness and respect, keeping a clear conscience.
1 Peter 3:15–16

My Relationships As a Christian Woman
How to Recognize a Good Church

They devoted themselves to the apostles' teaching and to the fellowship, to the breaking of bread and to prayer.

Acts 2:42

December 7

My Relationships As a Christian Woman
My Responsibilities to Individuals

Do not forget to entertain strangers, for by so doing some people have entertained angels without knowing it.

Hebrews 13:2

My Relationships As a Christian Woman
My Role in the Body of Christ

Therefore, I urge you, brothers, in view of God's mercy, to offer your bodies as living sacrifices, holy and pleasing to God—which is your spiritual worship.

Romans 12:1

December 6

My Relationships As a Christian Woman
My Responsibilities to the Poor

How long will you defend the unjust and show partiality to the wicked? Defend the cause of the weak and fatherless; maintain the rights of the poor and oppressed. Rescue the weak and needy; deliver them from the hand of the wicked.

Psalm 82:2–4

My Inner Life As a Christian Woman
How I Get the Most From Scripture

If anyone obeys his word, God's love is truly made complete in him.
1 John 2:5

My Identity As a Christian Woman
I Am Destined for Eternal Glory

*W*hen Christ, who is your life, appears, then you also will appear with him in glory.
Colossians 3:4

My Inner Life As a Christian Woman

How I Develop a Prayer Life

Trust in him at all times, O people; pour out your hearts to him, for God is our refuge.
Psalm 62:8

My Identity As a Christian Woman

I Am Guided Through Life

He guides the humble in what is right and teaches them his way.

Psalm 25:9

My Inner Life As a Christian Woman
How I Develop a Praise Life

I will praise you as long as I live, and in your name I will lift up my hands.
Psalm 63:4

My Identity As a Christian Woman
I Am Indwelt by God's Spirit

We have not received the spirit of the world but the Spirit who is from God, that we may understand what God has freely given us.

1 Corinthians 2:12

January 30

My Inner Life As a Christian Woman
How I Overcome Temptations

No temptation has seized you except what is common to man. And God is faithful; he will not let you be tempted beyond what you can bear. But when you are tempted, he will also provide a way out so that you can stand up under it.

1 Corinthians 10:13

My Identity As a Christian Woman

I Am Destined for Eternal Glory

The Lord Jesus (will be) revealed from heaven . . . he comes to be glorified in his holy people and to be marveled at among all those who have believed.

2 Thessalonians 1:7,10

January 31

My Inner Life As a Christian Woman
How I Deal With Pride

The arrogance of man will be brought low and the pride of men humbled; the LORD alone will be exalted in that day.

Isaiah 2:17

December 1

My Identity As a Christian Woman
I Am Growing More Christlike

Therefore, since Christ suffered in his body, arm yourselves also with the same attitude, because he who has suffered in his body is done with sin. As a result, he does not live the rest of his earthly life for evil human desires, but rather for the will of God.

1 Peter 4:1–2

February 1

My Identity As a Christian Woman
I Am Called to Be a Disciple

If anyone would come after me, he must deny himself and take up his cross and follow me. For whoever wants to save his life will lose it, but whoever loses his life for me will find it.

Matthew 16:24–25

My Inner Life As a Christian Woman

How I Deal With Loneliness

𝒟o not envy wicked men, do not desire their company.

Proverbs 24:1

My Identity As a Christian Woman
I Am Guided Through Life

Trust in the LORD with all your heart and lean not on your own understanding; in all your ways acknowledge him, and he will make your paths straight.

Proverbs 3:5–6

November 29

My Inner Life As a Christian Woman
How I Deal With Self-Doubt

Consider the ravens: They do not sow or reap, they have no storeroom or barn; yet God feeds them. And how much more valuable you are than birds!

Luke 12:24

February 3

My Identity As a Christian Woman

I Am Guarded by God's Power

Praise be to the God and Father of our Lord Jesus Christ! In his great mercy he has given us new birth into a living hope through the resurrection of Jesus Christ from the dead, and into an inheritance that can never perish, spoil or fade—kept in heaven for you, who through faith are shielded by God's power until the coming of the salvation that is ready to be revealed in the last time.

1 Peter 1:3–5

November 28

My Inner Life As a Christian Woman
How I Deal With Pride

Do not keep talking so proudly or let your mouth speak such arrogance, for the LORD is a God who knows, and by him deeds are weighed.

1 Samuel 2:3

February 4

My Identity As a Christian Woman
I Am Growing More Christlike

Those God foreknew he also predestined to be conformed to the likeness of his Son, that he might be the firstborn among many brothers.

Romans 8:29

November 27

My Inner Life As a Christian Woman

How I Develop a Praise Life

Ascribe to the LORD, O mighty ones, ascribe to the LORD glory and strength. Ascribe to the LORD the glory due his name; worship the LORD in the splendor of his holiness.

Psalm 29:1–2

My Identity As a Christian Woman

I Am Destined for Eternal Glory

But your dead will live; their bodies will rise. You who dwell in the dust, wake up and shout for joy. Your dew is like the dew of the morning; the earth will give birth to her dead.

Isaiah 26:19

November 26

My Inner Life As a Christian Woman

How I Develop a Prayer Life

So I say to you: "Ask, and it will be given to you; seek and you will find; knock and the door will be opened to you. For everyone who asks receives; he who seeks finds; and to him who knocks the door will be opened."

Luke 11:9–10

February 6

My Relationships As a Christian Woman
My Spiritual Gifts

Now to each one the manifestation of the Spirit is given for the common good. All these are the work of one and the same Spirit, and he gives them to each one, just as he determines.

1 Corinthians 12:7,11

November 25

My Relationships As a Christian Woman
My Relationships With Non-Christians

Live such good lives among the pagans that, though they accuse you of doing wrong, they may see your good deeds and glorify God on the day he visits us.

1 Peter 2:12

February 7

My Relationships As a Christian Woman
My Fellowship With Others

Live in harmony with one another. Do not be proud, but be willing to associate with people of low position. Do not be conceited.

Romans 12:16

November 24

My Relationships As a Christian Woman
My Attitude Toward Non-Christians

Give everyone what you owe him: If you owe taxes, pay taxes; if revenue, then revenue; if respect, then respect; if honor, then honor.

Romans 13:7

My Relationships As a Christian Woman
My Giving

*S*hare with God's people who are in need.

Romans 12:13

November 23

My Relationships As a Christian Woman
How Christian Values Differ

What is more, I consider everything a loss compared to the surpassing greatness of knowing Christ Jesus my Lord, for whose sake I have lost all things. I consider them rubbish, that I may gain Christ.

Philippians 3:8

February 9

My Relationships As a Christian Woman
My Attitudes Toward Others

Be devoted to one another in brotherly love. Honor one another above yourselves.
Romans 12:10

My Relationships As a Christian Woman
How to Enrich My Relationships

All of you, live in harmony with one another; be sympathetic, love as brothers, be compassionate and humble.

1 Peter 3:8

My Relationships As a Christian Woman
How to Be a Leader

*H*e tends his flock like a shepherd: He gathers the lambs in his arms and carries them close to his heart; he gently leads those that have young.

Isaiah 40:11

My Relationships As a Christian Woman
How to Enrich My Relationships

*H*e who conceals his sins does not prosper, but whoever confesses and renounces them finds mercy.

Proverbs 28:13

February 11

My Relationships As a Christian Woman
How to Relate to Leaders

Now we ask you, brothers, to respect those who work hard among you, who are over you in the Lord and who admonish you. Hold them in the highest regard in love because of their work.

1 Thessalonians 5:12–13

November 20

My Relationships As a Christian Woman
How to Relate to Leaders

*W*hoever humbles himself like this child is the greatest in the kingdom.
Matthew 18:4

My Relationships As a Christian Woman
How to Enrich My Relationships

Warn a divisive person once, and then warn him a second time. After that, have nothing to do with him.

Titus 3:10

My Relationships As a Christian Woman
My Attitudes Toward Others

We urge you, brothers, warn those who are idle, encourage the timid, help the weak, be patient with everyone.

1 Thessalonians 5:14

My Relationships As a Christian Woman

How to Enrich My Relationships

*L*et your gentleness be evident to all.

Philippians 4:5

November 18

My Relationships As a Christian Woman
My Giving

He who supplies seeds to the sower and bread for food will also supply and increase your store of seed and will enlarge the harvest of your righteousness. You will be made rich in every way so that you can be generous on every occasion, and through us your generosity will result in thanksgiving to God.

2 Corinthians 9:10–11

My Relationships As a Christian Woman
How Christian Values Differ

Acknowledge and take to heart this day that the LORD is God in heaven above and on the earth below. There is no other.

Deuteronomy 4:39

November 17

My Relationships As a Christian Woman
My Fellowship With Others

I urge you, brothers, to watch out for those who cause divisions and put obstacles in your way that are contrary to the teaching you have learned. Keep away from them.

Romans 16:17

February 15

My Relationships As a Christian Woman
My Attitude Toward the World

Do not love the world or anything in the world. If anyone loves the world, the love of the Father is not in him. For everything in the world—the cravings of sinful man, the lust of his eyes and the boasting of what he has and does—comes not from the Father but from the world.
1 John 2:15–16

My Relationships As a Christian Woman
My Spiritual Gifts

Serve wholeheartedly, as if you were serving the Lord, not men, because you know that the Lord will reward.

Ephesians 6:7–8

February 16

My Relationships As a Christian Woman
My Attitude Toward Non-Christians

Let no debt remain outstanding, except the continuing debt to love one another, for he who loves his fellow man has fulfilled the law.

Romans 13:8

My Relationships As a Christian Woman
My Role in the Body of Christ

I myself am convinced, my brothers, that you yourselves are full of goodness, complete in knowledge and competent to instruct one another.

Romans 15:14

My Relationships As a Christian Woman
My Relationships With Non-Christians

If you really keep the royal law found in Scripture, "Love your neighbor as yourself," you are doing right. But if you show favoritism, you sin and are convicted by the law as lawbreakers.

James 2:8–9

November 14

My Relationships As a Christian Woman

How to Recognize a Good Church

Though you have not seen him, you love him; and even though you do not see him now, you believe in him and are filled with an inexpressible and glorious joy, for you are receiving the goal of your faith, the salvation of your souls.

1 Peter 1:8–9

February 18

My Relationships As a Christian Woman
My Attitude Toward Materialism

I know what it is to be in need, and I know what it is to have plenty. I have learned the secret of being content in any and every situation, whether well fed or hungry, whether living in plenty or in want. I can do everything through him who gives me strength.

Philippians 4:12–13

November 13

My Relationships As a Christian Woman
How to Guide in Problem Situations

"*Lord*, how many times shall I forgive my brother when he sins against me? Up to seven times?" Jesus answered, "I tell you, not seven times, but seventy-seven times."

Matthew 18:21–22

February 19

My Relationships As a Christian Woman
My Responsibilities as a Citizen

Submit yourselves for the LORD's sake to every authority instituted among men: whether to the king, as the supreme authority, or to governors, who are sent by him to punish those who do wrong and to commend those who do right. For it is God's will that by doing good you should silence the ignorant talk of foolish men.

1 Peter 2:13–14

November 12

My Relationships As a Christian Woman
How to Guide in Problem Situations

Children, obey your parents in the Lord, for this is right. "Honor your father and mother"—which is the first commandment with a promise—"that it may go well with you and that you may enjoy long life on the earth."

Ephesians 6:1–3

February 20

My Relationships As a Christian Woman
My Responsibilities to the Poor

If a man shuts his ears to the cry of the poor, he too will cry out and not be answered.
Proverbs 21:13

My Relationships As a Christian Woman

How to Communicate Love

You are a forgiving God, gracious and compassionate, slow to anger and abounding in love.

Nehemiah 9:17

February 21

My Relationships As a Christian Woman
My Responsibilities to Individuals

Do not show partiality in judging; hear both small and great alike. Do not be afraid of any man, for judgment belongs to God.

Deuteronomy 1:17

November 10

My Relationships As a Christian Woman
How to Encourage Spiritual Growth

*L*ove the LORD your God with all your heart and with all your soul and with all your strength. These commandments that I give you today are to be upon your hearts. Impress them on your children. Talk about them.

Deuteronomy 6:5–7

February 22

My Relationships As a Christian Woman
How to Introduce a Person to Jesus

Do not be ashamed to testify about our Lord, or ashamed of me his prisoner. But join with me in suffering for the gospel, by the power of God.

2 Timothy 1:8

November 9

My Relationships As a Christian Woman
My Resources for Discipline

If we confess our sins, he is faithful and just to forgive us our sins and purify us from all unrighteousness.

1 John 1:9

February 23

My Relationships As a Christian Woman
My Attitude Toward Money

Better a little with righteousness than much gain with injustice.
Proverbs 16:8

My Relationships As a Christian Woman
My Purpose in Discipline

*D*o not withhold discipline from a child; if you punish him with the rod, he will not die. Punish him with the rod and save his soul from death.

Proverbs 23:13

February 24

My Relationships As a Christian Woman
My Attitude Toward Work

Our people must learn to devote themselves to doing what is good, in order that they may provide for daily necessities and not live unproductive lives.

Titus 3:14

November 7

My Relationships As a Christian Woman
My Goals in Child Rearing

From infancy you have known the holy Scriptures, which are able to make you wise for salvation through faith in Christ Jesus.

2 Timothy 3:15

My Inner Life As a Christian Woman

How I Deal With Self-Doubt

*H*is pleasure is not in the strength of the horse, nor his delight in the legs of a man; the LORD delights in those who fear him, who put their hope in his unfailing love.

Psalm 147:10–11

My Relationships As a Christian Woman

How to Mother

She speaks with wisdom, and faithful instruction is on her tongue. She watches over the affairs of her household and does not eat the bread of idleness. Her children arise and call her blessed; her husband also, he praises her. "Many women do noble things, but you surpass them all."

Proverbs 31:26–29

My Inner Life As a Christian Woman
How I Deal With Loneliness

*O*ffer hospitality to one another without grumbling.

1 Peter 4:9

My Identity As a Christian Woman
I Am Guarded by God's Power

Guard my life, for I am devoted to you. You are my God; save your servant who trusts in you.

Psalm 86:2

My Inner Life As a Christian Woman

How I Deal With Discouragement

Why are you downcast, O my soul? Why so disturbed within me? Put your hope in God, for I will yet praise him, my Savior and my God.

Psalm 42:11

My Identity As a Christian Woman

I Am Guided Through Life

For the LORD watches over the way of the righteous, but the way of the wicked will perish.

Psalm 1:6

February 28

My Inner Life As a Christian Woman
How I Channel My Thought Life

Finally, brothers, whatever is true, whatever is noble, whatever is right, whatever is pure, whatever is lovely, whatever is admirable—if anything is excellent or praiseworthy—think about such things.

Philippians 4:8

My Identity As a Christian Woman
I Am Indwelt by God's Spirit

May the God of hope fill you will all joy and peace as you trust in him, so that you may overflow with hope by the power of the Holy Spirit.

Romans 15:13

My Inner Life As a Christian Woman

How I Deal With Anxiety and Worry

Though the mountains be shaken and the hills be removed, yet my unfailing love for you will not be shaken nor my covenant of peace be removed.

Isaiah 54:10

November 2

My Identity As a Christian Woman
I Am Part of God's Family

No one who is born of God will continue to sin, because God's seed remains in him; he cannot go on sinning, because he has been born of God.

1 John 3:9

March 1

My Identity As a Christian Woman
I Am Created in God's Image

What is man that you are mindful of him? You made him ruler over the works of your hands; you put everything under his feet.

Psalm 8:4–6

My Identity As a Christian Woman
I Am Saved by Christ's Sacrifice

Who shall separate us from the love of Christ? Shall trouble or hardship or persecution or famine or nakedness or danger or sword? No, in all these things we are more than conquerors through him who loved us. For I am convinced that neither death nor life, neither angels nor demons . . . nor anything else in all creation, will be able to separate us from the love of God that is in Christ Jesus our Lord.

Romans 8:35,37–39

My Identity As a Christian Woman
I Am Saved by Christ's Sacrifice

I have been crucified with Christ and I no longer live, but Christ lives in me. The life I live in the body, I live by faith in the Son of God, who loved me and gave himself for me.

Galatians 2:20

October 31

My Inner Life As a Christian Woman
How I Get the Most From Scripture

Why do you call me, "Lord, Lord" and do not do what I say?

Luke 6:46

My Identity As a Christian Woman
I Am Part of God's Family

Can a mother forget the baby at her breast and have no compassion on the child she has borne? Though she may forget, I will not forget you!

Isaiah 49:15

My Inner Life As a Christian Woman

How I Deal With Anxiety and Worry

The LORD is a refuge for the oppressed, a stronghold in times of trouble.
Psalm 9:9

March 4

My Identity As a Christian Woman
I Am Indwelt by God's Spirit

The Father . . . will give you another Counselor to be with you forever—the Spirit of truth.

John 14:16–17

October 29

My Inner Life As a Christian Woman
How I Channel My Thought Life

Turn my eyes away from worthless things; renew my life according to your word.
Psalm 119:37

March 5

My Identity As a Christian Woman
I Am Gifted to Serve Others

Just as each of us has one body with many members, and these members do not all have the same function, so in Christ we who are many form one body, and each member belongs to all the others. We have different gifts, according to the grace given us.

Romans 12:4–6

My Inner Life As a Christian Woman

How I Deal With Discouragement

Even youths grow tired and weary, and young men stumble and fall; but those who hope in the LORD will renew their strength.

Isaiah 40:30–31

March 6

My Relationships As a Christian Woman
God's Ideal for My Marriage

Isaac brought her into the tent of his mother Sarah, and he married Rebekah. So she became his wife, and he loved her; and Isaac was comforted after his mother's death.

Genesis 24:67

October 27

My Inner Life As a Christian Woman
How I Deal With Loneliness

Jesus said to his host, "When you give a luncheon or dinner, do not invite your friends, your brothers or relatives, or your rich neighbors; if you do, they may invite you back and so you will be repaid. But when you give a banquet, invite the poor, the crippled, the lame, the blind, and you will be blessed. Although they cannot repay you, you will be repaid at the resurrection of the righteous."

Luke 14:12–14

March 7

My Relationships As a Christian Woman
My Role as a Wife

Her husband has full confidence in her and lacks nothing of value. She brings him good, not harm, all the days of her life. . . . Charm is deceptive, and beauty is fleeting; but a woman who fears the LORD is to be praised. Give her the reward she has earned, and let her works bring her praise at the city gate.

Proverbs 31:11–12, 30–31

October 26

My Relationships As a Christian Woman
My Attitude Toward Forgiveness

This is what the Sovereign LORD, the Holy One of Israel, says: "In repentance and rest is your salvation, in quietness and trust is your strength."

Isaiah 30:15

March 8

My Relationships As a Christian Woman
My Attitude Toward Sex

For everything God created is good, and nothing is to be rejected if it is received with thanksgiving, because it is consecrated by the word of God and prayer.

1 Timothy 4:4–5

October 25

My Relationships As a Christian Woman
My Attitude Toward Openness

Therefore each of you must put off falsehood and speak truthfully to his neighbor, for we are all members of one body.

Ephesians 4:25

March 9

My Relationships As a Christian Woman
My Approach to Conflict

The wisdom that comes from heaven is first of all pure; then peace loving, considerate, submissive, full of mercy and good fruit, impartial and sincere. Peacemakers who sow in peace raise a harvest of righteousness.

James 3:17–18

October 24

My Relationships As a Christian Woman
My Approach to Weakness

Do not judge, or you too will be judged. For in the same way you judge others, you will be judged, and with the measure you use, it will be measured to you.

Matthew 7:1–2

My Relationships As a Christian Woman
My Approach to Hurt

Let us not become weary in doing good, for at the proper time we will reap a harvest if we do not give up.

Galatians 6:9

October 23

My Relationships As a Christian Woman
My Approach to Anger

Do not judge, and you will not be judged. Do not condemn, and you will not be condemned. Forgive, and you will be forgiven.

Luke 6:37

March 11

My Relationships As a Christian Woman

My Approach to Anger

Refrain from anger and turn from wrath; do not fret—it leads only to evil.
Psalm 37:8

October 22

My Relationships As a Christian Woman

My Approach to Hurt

If you are offering your gift at the altar and there remember that your brother has something against you, leave your gift there in front of the altar. First go and be reconciled to your brother; then come and offer your gift.

Matthew 5:23–24

March 12

My Relationships As a Christian Woman
My Approach to Weakness

Why do you look at the speck of sawdust in your brother's eye and pay no attention to the plank in your own eye? How can you say to your brother "Let me take the speck out of your eye," when all the time there is a plank in your own eye?

Matthew 7:3–4

October 21

My Relationships As a Christian Woman
My Approach to Conflict

Make my joy complete by being like-minded, having the same love, being one in spirit and purpose.

Philippians 2:2

March 13

My Relationships As a Christian Woman
My Attitude Toward Openness

Therefore confess your sins to each other and pray for each other so that you may be healed.

James 5:16

October 20

My Relationships As a Christian Woman
My Attitude Toward Sex

How beautiful you are and how pleasing, O love, with your delights! Your stature is like that of the palm, and your breasts like clusters of fruit. I said, "I will climb the palm tree; I will take hold of its fruit."

Song of Songs 7:6–8

My Relationships As a Christian Woman
My Attitude Toward Forgiveness

*I*f you, O LORD, kept a record of sins, O LORD, who could stand? But with you there is forgiveness; therefore you are feared.

Psalm 130:3–4

October 19

My Relationships As a Christian Woman
My Attitude Toward Work

All hard work brings a profit, but mere talk leads only to poverty.
Proverbs 14:23

March 15

My Relationships As a Christian Woman
How to Mother

Only be careful, and watch yourselves closely so that you do not forget the things your eyes have seen or let them slip from your heart as long as you live. Teach them to your children and to their children after them.

Deuteronomy 4:9

October 18

My Relationships As a Christian Woman
My Attitude Toward Money

Remember the LORD your God, for it is he who gives you the ability to produce wealth.
Deuteronomy 8:18

March 16

My Relationships As a Christian Woman
My Goals in Child Rearing

For attaining wisdom and discipline; for understanding words of insight; for acquiring a disciplined and prudent life, doing what is right and just and fair.

Proverbs 1:2–3

My Relationships As a Christian Woman
How to Introduce a Person to Jesus

For it is by grace you have been saved, through faith—and this not from yourselves, it is the gift of God—not by works, so that no one can boast.

Ephesians 2:8–9

March 17

My Relationships As a Christian Woman
My Purpose in Discipline

My son, do not despise the LORD's discipline and do not resent his rebuke, because the LORD disciplines those he loves, as a father the son he delights in.

Proverbs 3:11–12

October 16

My Relationships As a Christian Woman
My Responsibilities to Individuals

Do not seek revenge or bear a grudge against one of your people, but love your neighbor as yourself. I am the LORD.

Leviticus 19:18

March 18

My Relationships As a Christian Woman
My Resources for Discipline

An anxious heart weighs a man down, but a kind word cheers him up.
Proverbs 12:25

October 15

My Relationships As a Christian Woman
My Responsibilities to the Poor

All they asked was that we should continue to remember the poor, the very thing I was eager to do.

Galatians 2:10

March 19

My Relationships As a Christian Woman
How to Encourage Spiritual Growth

Therefore let us stop passing judgment on one another. Instead, make up your mind not to put any stumbling block or obstacle in your brother's way.

Romans 14:13

October 14

My Relationships As a Christian Woman
My Responsibilities as a Citizen

I urge, then, first of all, that requests, prayers, intercession and thanksgiving be made for everyone—for kings and all those in authority, that we may live peaceful and quiet lives in all godliness and holiness.

1 Timothy 2:1–2

March 20

My Relationships As a Christian Woman
How to Pray for My Children

I pray also that the eyes of your heart may be enlightened in order that you may know the hope to which he has called you, the riches of his glorious inheritance in the saints, and his incomparably great power for us who believe.

Ephesians 1:18–19

My Relationships As a Christian Woman
My Relationships With Non-Christians

Don't have anything to do with foolish and stupid arguments, because you know they produce quarrels.

2 Timothy 2:23–24

March 21

My Relationships As a Christian Woman
How to Communicate Love

Dear children, let us not love with words or tongue but with actions and in truth.
1 John 3:18

October 12

My Relationships As a Christian Woman
My Attitude Toward Non-Christians

Do not be overawed when a man grows rich, when the splendor of his house increases; for he will take nothing with him when he dies, his splendor will not descend with him.

Psalm 49:16–17

March 22

My Relationships As a Christian Woman
How to Tell My Child About God

When your children ask you, "What does this ceremony mean to you" then tell them.
Exodus 12:26

October 11

My Relationships As a Christian Woman
My Attitude Toward the World

God chose the lowly things of this world and the despised things—and the things that are not—to nullify the things that are, so that no one may boast before him.

1 Corinthians 1:28

March 23

My Relationships As a Christian Woman
How to Guide in Problem Situations

Whoever of you loves life and desires to see many good days, keep your tongue from evil and your lips from speaking lies.

Psalm 34:12–13

October 10

My Relationships As a Christian Woman
How Christian Values Differ

I want to know Christ and the power of his resurrection and the fellowship of sharing in his sufferings, becoming like him in his death.

Philippians 3:10

March 24

My Relationships As a Christian Woman
How to Guide in Problem Situations

A gentle answer turns away wrath, but a harsh word stirs up anger.
Proverbs 15:1

October 9

My Relationships As a Christian Woman
How to Enrich My Relationships

*C*onsider the blameless, observe the upright; there is a future for the man of peace.
Psalm 37:37

March 25

My Relationships As a Christian Woman
How to Recognize a Good Church

Sing to him, sing praise to him; tell of all his wonderful acts. Glory in his holy name; let the hearts of those who seek the LORD rejoice.

Psalm 105:2–3

My Relationships As a Christian Woman

How to Enrich My Relationships

Rather, we have renounced secret and shameful ways; we do not use deception, nor do we distort the word of God. On the contrary, by setting forth the truth plainly we commend ourselves to every man's conscience in the sight of God.

2 Corinthians 4:2

March 26

My Relationships As a Christian Woman
My Role in the Body of Christ

Let us consider how we may spur one another on toward love and good deeds. Let us not give up meeting together, as some are in the habit of doing, but let us encourage one another—and all the more as you see the Day approaching.

Hebrews 10:24–25

October 7

My Relationships As a Christian Woman
How to Relate to Leaders

Obey your leaders and submit to their authority. They keep watch over you as men who must give an account. Obey them so that their work will be a joy, not a burden, for that would be of no advantage to you.

Hebrews 13:17

March 27

My Inner Life As a Christian Woman
How I Get the Most From Scripture

The law of the LORD is perfect, reviving the soul. The statutes of the LORD are trustworthy, making wise the simple. The precepts of the LORD are right, giving joy to the heart. The commands of the LORD are radiant, giving light to the eyes. The fear of the LORD is pure, enduring forever.

Psalm 19:7–9

October 6

My Relationships As a Christian Woman

How to Be a Leader

The fear of the LORD teaches a man wisdom, and humility comes before honor.
Proverbs 15:33

March 28

My Inner Life As a Christian Woman
How I Develop a Prayer Life

Listen to my cry for help, my King and my God, for to you I pray. Morning by morning, O LORD, you hear my voice; morning by morning I lay my requests before you and wait in expectation.

Psalm 5:2–3

My Identity As a Christian Woman
I Am Created in God's Image

Be holy because I, the LORD your God, am holy.

Leviticus 19:2

March 29

My Inner Life As a Christian Woman
How I Develop a Praise Life

May all who seek you rejoice and be glad in you; may those who love your salvation always say, "Let God be exalted."

Psalm 70:4

October 4

My Identity As a Christian Woman
I Am Destined for Eternal Glory

We make it our goal to please him . . . for we must all appear before the judgment seat of Christ, that each one may receive what is due him.

2 Corinthians 5:9–10

March 30

My Inner Life As a Christian Woman
How I Overcome Temptations

*I*f any of you lacks wisdom, he should ask God, who gives generously to all without finding fault, and it will be given to him.

James 1:5

October 3

My Identity As a Christian Woman
I Am Growing More Christlike

You are a letter from Christ, the result of our ministry, written not with ink but with the Spirit of the living God, not on tablets of stone but on tablets of human hearts.

2 Corinthians 3:3

March 31

My Inner Life As a Christian Woman
How I Deal With Pride

This is what the LORD says: "Let not the wise man boast of his wisdom or the strong man boast of his strength or the rich man boast of his riches, but let him who boasts boast about this: that he understands and knows me, that I am the LORD, who exercises kindness, justice and righteousness on earth, for in these I delight."

Jeremiah 9:23–24

My Identity As a Christian Woman
I Am Guarded by God's Power

He who dwells in the shelter of the Most High will rest in the shadow of the Almighty. I will say of the LORD, "He is my refuge and my fortress, my God, in whom I trust."

Psalm 91:1–2

April 1

My Identity As a Christian Woman
I Am Called to Be a Disciple

To the Jews who had believed him, Jesus said, "If you hold to my teaching, you are really my disciples. Then you will know the truth, and the truth will set you free."

John 8:31–32

October 1

My Identity As a Christian Woman

I Am Guided Through Life

Delight yourself in the LORD and he will give you the desires of your heart.
Psalm 37:4

April 2

My Identity As a Christian Woman
I Am Guided Through Life

In your unfailing love you will lead the people you have redeemed. In your strength you will guide them to your holy dwelling.

Exodus 15:13

September 30

My Inner Life As a Christian Woman

How I Deal With Self-Doubt

I am still confident of this: I will see the goodness of the LORD in the land of the living. Wait for the LORD; be strong and take heart and wait for the LORD.

Psalm 27:13–14

April 3

My Identity As a Christian Woman
I Am Guarded by God's Power

Even to your old age and gray hairs I am he, I am he who will sustain you. I have made you. . . . I will sustain you and I will rescue you.

Isaiah 46:4

My Inner Life As a Christian Woman
How I Deal With Pride

$\mathcal{W}$ho makes you different from anyone else? What do you have that you did not receive? And if you did receive it, why do you boast as though you did not?

1 Corinthians 4:7

April 4

My Identity As a Christian Woman
I Am Growing More Christlike

Put to death, therefore, whatever belongs to your earthly nature: . . . you have taken off your old self with its practices and have put on the new self, which is being renewed in knowledge in the image of its Creator.

Colossians 3:5,9–10

September 28

My Inner Life As a Christian Woman
How I Develop a Praise Life

No one is like you, O LORD; you are great, and your name is mighty in power. Who would not revere you, O King of the nations? This is your due. Among all the wise men of the nations and in all their kingdoms, there is no one like you.

Jeremiah 10:6–7

April 5

My Identity As a Christian Woman
I Am Destined for Eternal Glory

So will it be with the resurrection of the dead. The body that is sown is perishable, it is raised imperishable; it is sown in dishonor, it is raised in glory; it is sown in weakness, it is raised in power; it is sown a natural body, it is raised a spiritual body.

1 Corinthians 15:42–44

September 27

My Inner Life As a Christian Woman
How I Develop a Prayer Life

Be joyful always; pray continually; give thanks in all circumstances, for this is God's will for you in Christ Jesus.

1 Thessalonians 5:16–18

April 6

My Relationships As a Christian Woman
My Spiritual Gifts

I long to see you so that I may impart to you some spiritual gift to make you strong—that is, that you and I may be mutually encouraged by each other's faith.

Romans 1:11–12

September 26

My Inner Life As a Christian Woman
How I Get the Most From Scripture

Everyone who hears these words of mine and puts them into practice is like a wise man who built his house on the rock. The rain came down, the streams rose, and the winds blew and beat against that house; yet it did not fall, because it had its foundations on the rock.

Matthew 7:24–25

April 7

My Relationships As a Christian Woman
My Fellowship With Others

If two of you on earth agree about anything you ask for, it will be done for you by my Father in heaven. For where two or three come together in my name, there am I with them.

Matthew 18:19–20

September 25

My Relationships As a Christian Woman
My Attitudes Toward Others

The man who eats everything must not look down on him who does not, and the man who does not eat everything must not condemn the man who does, for God has accepted him. Who are you to judge someone else's servant? To his master he stands or falls. And he will stand, for the Lord is able to make him stand.

Romans 14:3–4

April 8

My Relationships As a Christian Woman
My Giving

If anyone has material possessions and sees his brother in need but has no pity on him, how can the love of God be in him? Dear children, let us not love with words or tongue but with actions and in truth.

1 John 3:17–18

My Relationships As a Christian Woman
My Giving

Each man should give what he had decided in his heart to give, not reluctantly or under compulsion, for God loves a cheerful giver.

2 Corinthians 9:7

April 9

My Relationships As a Christian Woman
My Attitudes Toward Others

Do not rebuke an older man harshly, but exhort him as if he were your father. Treat younger men as brothers, older women as mothers, and younger women as sisters, with absolute purity.

1 Timothy 5:1–2

September 23

My Relationships As a Christian Woman
My Fellowship With Others

May the God who gives endurance and encouragement give you a spirit of unity among yourselves as you follow Christ Jesus, so that with one heart and mouth you may glorify the God and Father of our Lord Jesus Christ.

Romans 15:5–6

April 10

My Relationships As a Christian Woman
How to Be a Leader

Jesus called them together and said, "You know that the rulers of the Gentiles lord it over them, and their high officials exercise authority over them. No so with you. Instead, whoever wants to become great among you must be your servant, and whoever wants to be first must be your slave—just as the Son of Man did not come to be served, but to serve, and to give his life a ransom for many."

Matthew 20:25–28

September 22

My Relationships As a Christian Woman
My Spiritual Gifts

This is a trustworthy saying. And I want you to stress these things, so that those who have trusted in God may be careful to devote themselves to doing what is good. These things are excellent and profitable for all.

Titus 3:8

April 11

My Relationships As a Christian Woman
How to Relate to Leaders

Do not entertain an accusation against an elder unless it is brought by two or three witnesses. Those who sin are to be rebuked publicly, so that the others may take warning.

1 Timothy 5:19–20

My Relationships As a Christian Woman
My Role in the Body of Christ

Do not forget to do good and to share with others, for with such sacrifices God is pleased.

Hebrews 13:16

April 12

My Relationships As a Christian Woman
How to Enrich My Relationships

Do not repay anyone evil for evil. Be careful to do what is right in the eyes of everybody.
Romans 12:17

September 20

My Relationships As a Christian Woman
How to Recognize a Good Church

Do not merely listen to the word, and so deceive yourselves. Do what it says.
James 1:22

April 13

My Relationships As a Christian Woman
How to Enrich My Relationships

Accept one another, then, just as Christ accepted you, in order to bring praise to God.
Romans 15:7

My Relationships As a Christian Woman
How to Guide in Problem Situations

Fear of man will prove to be a snare, but whoever trusts in the LORD is kept safe.
Proverbs 29:25

April 14

My Relationships As a Christian Woman
How Christian Values Differ

But you, man of God . . . pursue righteousness, godliness, faith, love, endurance and gentleness.

1 Timothy 6:11

My Relationships As a Christian Woman
How to Guide in Problem Situations

My son, if sinners entice you, do not give in to them.

Proverbs 1:10

April 15

My Relationships As a Christian Woman
My Attitude Toward the World

Do not conform any longer to the pattern of this world, but be transformed by the renewing of your mind. Then you will be able to test and approve what God's will is—his good, pleasing and perfect will.

Romans 12:2

My Relationships As a Christian Woman
How to Tell My Child About God

Be careful, and watch yourselves closely so that you do not forget the things your eyes have seen or let them slip from your heart as long as you live. Teach them to your children and to their children after them.

Deuteronomy 4:9–10

April 16

My Relationships As a Christian Woman
My Attitude Toward Non-Christians

Do not be yoked together with unbelievers. For what do righteousness and wickedness have in common? Or what fellowship can light have with darkness?

2 Corinthians 6:14

My Relationships As a Christian Woman

How to Communicate Love

Solomon showed his love for the LORD by walking according to the statutes of his father David.

1 Kings 3:3

My Relationships As a Christian Woman
My Relationships With Non-Christians

Let your light shine before men, that they may see your good deeds and praise your Father in heaven.

Matthew 5:16

September 15

My Relationships As a Christian Woman
How to Pray for My Children

This is my prayer: that your love may abound more and more in knowledge and depth of insight, so that you may be able to discern what is best and may be pure and blameless until the day of Christ.

Philippians 1:9–10

April 18

My Relationships As a Christian Woman
My Attitude Toward Materialism

Be careful that you do not forget the LORD your God, failing to observe his commands, his laws and his decrees that I am giving you this day. Otherwise, when you eat and are satisfied, when you build fine houses and settle down, and when your herds and flocks grow large and your silver and gold increase and all you have is multiplied, then your heart will become proud and you will forget the LORD your God, who brought you out of Egypt, out of the land of slavery.

Deuteronomy 8:11–14

My Relationships As a Christian Woman
How to Encourage Spiritual Growth

Let us consider how we may spur one another on toward love and good deeds. Let us not give up meeting together, as some are in the habit of doing, but let us encourage one another—and all the more as you see the Day approaching.

Hebrews 10:24–25

April 19

My Relationships As a Christian Woman
My Responsibilities as a Citizen

Everyone must submit himself to the governing authorities, for there is no authority except that which God established.

Romans 13:1

My Relationships As a Christian Woman
My Resources for Discipline

Folly is bound up in the heart of a child, but the rod of discipline will drive it far from him.

Proverbs 22:15

April 20

My Relationships As a Christian Woman
My Responsibilities to the Poor

Woe to those who make unjust laws, to those who issue oppressive decrees, to deprive the poor of their rights and rob my oppressed people of justice, making widows their prey and robbing the fatherless.

Isaiah 10:1–2

September 12

My Relationships As a Christian Woman
My Purpose in Discipline

When we are judged by the Lord, we are being disciplined so that we will not be condemned with the world.

1 Corinthians 11:32

April 21

My Relationships As a Christian Woman
My Responsibilities to Individuals

I pray that you may be active in sharing your faith, so that you will have a full understanding of every good thing we have in Christ.

Philemon 1:6

My Relationships As a Christian Woman
My Goals in Child Rearing

Don't let anyone look down on you because you are young, but set an example for the believers in speech, in life, in love, in faith, and in purity.

1 Timothy 4:12

April 22

My Relationships As a Christian Woman
How to Introduce a Person to Jesus

Surely the arm of the LORD is not too short to save, nor his ear too dull to hear. But your iniquities have separated you from your God; your sins have hidden his face from you, so that he will not hear.

Isaiah 59:1–2

September 10

My Relationships As a Christian Woman

How to Mother

So do not throw away your confidence; it will be richly rewarded. You need to persevere so that when you have done the will of God, you will receive what he has promised.
Hebrews 10:35–36

April 23

My Relationships As a Christian Woman
My Attitude Toward Money

People who want to get rich fall into temptation and a trap and into many foolish and harmful desires that plunge men into ruin and destruction. For the love of money is a root of all kinds of evil. Some people, eager for money, have wandered from the faith and pierced themselves with many griefs.

1 Timothy 6:9–10

My Relationships As a Christian Woman
My Attitude Toward Forgiveness

Her many sins have been forgiven—for she loved much. But he who has been forgiven little loves little.

Luke 7:47

April 24

My Relationships As a Christian Woman
My Attitude Toward Work

Make it your ambition to lead a quiet life, to mind your own business and to work with your hands, just as we told you, so that your daily life may win the respect of outsiders and so that you will not be dependent on anybody.

1 Thessalonians 4:11–12

September 8

My Relationships As a Christian Woman
My Attitude Toward Openness

Nothing in all creation is hidden from God's sight. Everything is uncovered and laid bare before the eyes of him to whom we must give account.

Hebrews 4:13

April 25

My Relationships As a Christian Woman
God's Ideal for My Marriage

In the Lord, however, woman is not independent of man, nor is man independent of woman. For as woman came from man, so also man is born of woman. But everything comes from God.

1 Corinthians 11:11–12

September 7

My Relationships As a Christian Woman
My Approach to Weakness

If you had known what these words mean, "I desire mercy, not sacrifice," you would not have condemned the innocent.

Matthew 12:7

April 26

My Inner Life As a Christian Woman
How I Deal With Self-Doubt

He will be a sure foundation for your times, a rich store of salvation and wisdom and knowledge; the fear of the LORD is the key to this treasure.

Isaiah 33:6

September 6

My Relationships As a Christian Woman

My Approach to Anger

Who is a God like you, who pardons sin and forgives the transgression of the remnant of his inheritance? You do not stay angry forever but delight to show mercy. You will again have compassion on us; you will tread our sins underfoot and hurl all our iniquities into the depths of the sea.

Micah 7:18–19

April 27

My Inner Life As a Christian Woman

How I Deal With Loneliness

Rejoice with those who rejoice, mourn with those who mourn.

Romans 12:15

September 5

My Identity As a Christian Woman
I Am Called to Be a Disciple

I am the vine; you are the branches. If a man remains in me and I in him, he will bear much fruit.... If you remain in me and my words remain in you, ask whatever you wish, and it will be given you. This is to my Father's glory, that you bear much fruit, showing yourselves to be my disciples.

John 15:5,7–8

My Inner Life As a Christian Woman
How I Deal With Discouragement

I will be glad and rejoice in your love, for you saw my affliction and knew the anguish of my soul.

Psalm 31:7

September 4

My Identity As a Christian Woman
I Am Indwelt by God's Spirit

So I say, live by the Spirit, and you will not gratify the desires of the sinful nature.
Galatians 5:16

April 29

My Inner Life As a Christian Woman
How I Channel My Thought Life

You will keep in perfect peace him whose mind is steadfast, because he trusts in you.
Isaiah 26:3

My Identity As a Christian Woman
I Am Part of God's Family

As obedient children, do not conform to the evil desires you had when you lived in ignorance. But just as he who called you is holy, so be holy in all you do; for it is written: "Be holy, because I am holy."

I Peter 1:14–16

My Inner Life As a Christian Woman

How I Deal With Anxiety and Worry

And my God will meet all your needs according to his glorious riches in Christ Jesus.
Philippians 4:19

September 2

My Identity As a Christian Woman

I Am Saved by Christ's Sacrifice

Now he has reconciled you by Christ's physical body through death to present you holy in his sight, without blemish and free from accusation.

Colossians 1:22

May 1

My Identity As a Christian Woman
I Am Created in God's Image

Know that the LORD is God. It is he who made us, and we are his; we are his people, the sheep of his pasture.

Psalm 100:3

September 1

My Identity As a Christian Woman
I Am Created in God's Image

You created my inmost being; you knit me together in my mother's womb. I praise you because I am fearfully and wonderfully made; your works are wonderful, I know that full well. My frame was not hidden from you when I was made in the secret place. When I was woven together in the depths of the earth, your eyes saw my unformed body. All the days ordained for me were written in your book before one of them came to be.

Psalm 139:13–16

May 2

My Identity As a Christian Woman
I Am Saved by Christ's Sacrifice

He who did not spare his own Son, but gave him up for us all—how will he not also, along with him, graciously give us all things?

Romans 8:32

My Inner Life As a Christian Woman
How I Deal With Anxiety and Worry

When I am afraid, I will trust in you. In God, whose word I praise, in God I trust; I will not be afraid. What can mortal man do to me?

Psalm 56:3–4

May 3

My Identity As a Christian Woman
I Am Part of God's Family

You are all sons of God through faith in Christ Jesus, for all of you who were baptized into Christ have clothed yourselves with Christ. There is neither Jew nor Greek, slave nor free, male nor female, for you are all one in Christ Jesus.

Galatians 3:26–28

My Inner Life As a Christian Woman
How I Channel My Thought Life

To the pure, all things are pure, but to those who are corrupted and do not believe, nothing is pure. In fact, both their minds and consciences are corrupted.

Titus 1:15

May 4

My Identity As a Christian Woman
I Am Indwelt by God's Spirit

The Spirit helps us in our weakness. We do not know what we ought to pray, but the Spirit himself intercedes for us with groans that words cannot express.

Romans 8:26

August 29

My Inner Life As a Christian Woman
How I Deal With Discouragement

For this very reason, make every effort to add to your faith goodness; and to goodness, knowledge; and to knowledge, self-control; and to self-control, perseverance; and to perseverance, godliness; and to godliness, brotherly kindness; and to brotherly kindness, love. If you possess these qualities in increasing measure, they will keep you from being ineffective and unproductive in your knowledge of our Lord Jesus Christ.

2 Peter 1:5–8

May 5

My Identity As a Christian Woman
I Am Gifted to Serve Others

Each one should use whatever gift he has received to serve others, faithfully administering God's grace in its various forms. If anyone speaks, he should do it as one speaking the very words of God. If anyone serves, he should do it with the strength God provides, so that in all things God may be praised through Jesus Christ.

I Peter 4:10–11

My Inner Life As a Christian Woman
How I Deal With Loneliness

God sets the lonely in families, he leads forth the prisoners with singing; but the rebellious live in a sun-scorched land.

Psalm 68:6

May 6

My Relationships As a Christian Woman
My Role as a Wife

Each one of you also must love his wife as he loves himself, and the wife must respect her husband.

Ephesians 5:33

August 27

My Inner Life As a Christian Woman
How I Deal With Self-Doubt

The LORD will guide you always; he will satisfy your needs in a sun-scorched land and will strengthen your frame. You will be like a well watered garden, like a spring whose waters never fail.

Isaiah 58:11

May 7

My Relationships As a Christian Woman
My Attitude Toward Sex

Marriage should be honored by all, and the marriage bed kept pure.
Hebrews 13:4

August 26

My Relationships As a Christian Woman

My Approach to Hurt

May the Lord make your love increase and overflow for each other and for everyone else, just as ours does for you.

1 Thessalonians 3:12

My Relationships As a Christian Woman
My Approach to Conflict

Let the word of Christ dwell in you richly as you teach and admonish one another with all wisdom.

Colossians 3:16

August 25

My Relationships As a Christian Woman
My Approach to Conflict

You are still worldly. For since there is jealousy and quarreling among you, are you not worldly? Are you not acting like mere men?

1 Corinthians 3:3

May 9

My Relationships As a Christian Woman
My Approach to Hurt

Do to others as you would have them do to you.

Luke 6:31

August 24

My Relationships As a Christian Woman
My Attitude Toward Sex

How delightful is your love, my sister, my bride! How much more pleasing is your love than wine, and the fragrance of your perfume than any spice! Your lips drop sweetness as the honeycomb, my bride; milk and honey are under your tongue. You are a garden fountain, a well of flowing water streaming down from Lebanon.

Song of Songs 4:10–11,15

May 10

My Relationships As a Christian Woman
My Approach to Anger

"In a surge of anger I hid my face from you for a moment, but with everlasting kindness I will have compassion on you," says the LORD your Redeemer.

Isaiah 54:8

August 23

My Relationships As a Christian Woman
My Role as a Wife

Wives, in the same way be submissive to your husbands so that, if any of them do not believe the word, they may be won over without talk by the behavior of their wives, when they see the purity and reverence of your lives.

1 Peter 3:1–2

My Relationships As a Christian Woman
My Approach to Weakness

He gives strength to the weary and increases the power of the weak.
Isaiah 40:29

August 22

My Relationships As a Christian Woman
My Attitude Toward Work

He who works his land will have abundant food, but the one who chases fantasies will have his fill of poverty.

Proverbs 28:19

May 12

My Relationships As a Christian Woman
My Attitude Toward Openness

No one who practices deceit will dwell in my house; no one who speaks falsely will stand in my presence.

Psalm 101:7

August 21

My Relationships As a Christian Woman
My Attitude Toward Money

Honor the LORD with your wealth, with the first fruits of all your crops; then your barns will be filled to overflowing, and your vats will brim over with new wine.

Proverbs 3:9–10

May 13

My Relationships As a Christian Woman
My Attitude Toward Forgiveness

If you forgive men when they sin against you, your heavenly Father will also forgive you. But if you do not forgive men their sins, your Father will not forgive your sins.

Matthew 6:14–15

August 20

My Relationships As a Christian Woman

How to Introduce a Person to Jesus

Jesus said to her, "I am the resurrection and the life. He who believes in me will live, even though he dies; and whoever lives and believes in me will never die."

John 11:25–26

May 14

My Relationships As a Christian Woman

How to Mother

Choose life, so that you and your children may live and that you may love the LORD your God, listen to his voice, and hold fast to him.

Deuteronomy 30:19–20

August 19

My Relationships As a Christian Woman
My Responsibilities to Individuals

Remember those in prison as if you were their fellow prisoners, and those who are mistreated as if you yourselves were suffering.

Hebrews 13:3

May 15

My Relationships As a Christian Woman
My Goals in Child Rearing

"Teacher, which is the greatest commandment in the Law?" Jesus replied, " 'Love the Lord your God with all your heart and with all your soul and with all your mind.' This is the first and greatest commandment. And the second is like it: 'Love your neighbor as yourself.' All the Law and the Prophets hang on these two commandments."

Matthew 22:36–41

My Relationships As a Christian Woman
My Responsibilities to the Poor

There will always be poor people in the land. Therefore I command you to be openhanded toward your brothers and toward the poor and needy in your land.

Deuteronomy 15:11

May 16

My Relationships As a Christian Woman
My Purpose in Discipline

You rebuke and discipline men for their sin.

Psalm 39:11

My Relationships As a Christian Woman
My Responsibilities as a Citizen

Remind the people to be subject to rulers and authorities, to be obedient, to be ready to do whatever is good.

Titus 3:1

My Relationships As a Christian Woman
My Resources for Discipline

Rebuke your neighbor frankly so you will not share in his guilt.
Leviticus 19:17

August 16

My Relationships As a Christian Woman
My Attitude Toward Materialism

Do not worry, saying, "What shall we eat?" or "What shall we drink?" or "What shall we wear?" For the pagans run after all these things, and your heavenly Father knows that you need them. But seek first his kingdom and his righteousness, and all these things will be given to you as well.

Matthew 6:31–33

My Relationships As a Christian Woman
How to Encourage Spiritual Growth

Let love and faithfulness never leave you; bind them around your neck, write them on the tablet of your heart. Then you will win favor and a good name.

Proverbs 3:3–4

My Relationships As a Christian Woman
My Relationships With Non-Christians

But love your enemies, do good to them, and lend to them without expecting to get anything back. Then your reward will be great, and you will be sons of the Most High, because he is kind to the ungrateful and wicked. Be merciful, just as your Father is merciful.

Luke 6:35–36

My Relationships As a Christian Woman
How to Pray for My Children

I pray that out of his glorious riches he may strengthen you with power through his spirit in your inner being, so that Christ may dwell in your hearts through faith.

Ephesians 3:16–17

August 14

My Relationships As a Christian Woman
My Attitude Toward Non-Christians

I have written you in my letter not to associate with sexually immoral people—not at all meaning the people of this world who are immoral, or the greedy and swindlers, or idolaters. In that case you would have to leave this world.

1 Corinthians 5:9–10

May 20

My Relationships As a Christian Woman

How to Communicate Love

As for me, far be it from me that I should sin against the LORD by failing to pray for you. And I will teach you the way that is good and right.

1 Samuel 12:23

August 13

My Relationships As a Christian Woman
My Attitude Toward the World

The world and its desires pass away, but the man who does the will of God lives forever.
1 John 2:17

May 21

My Relationships As a Christian Woman
How to Tell My Child About God

*L*ove the LORD your God with all your heart and with all your soul and with all your strength. These commandments that I give you today are to be upon your hearts. Impress them on your children. Talk about them when you sit at home and when you walk along the road, when you lie down and when you get up. . . . Write them on the door frames of your houses and on your gates.

Deuteronomy 7:5–7, 9

August 12

My Relationships As a Christian Woman
How Christian Values Differ

And now, O Israel, what does the LORD your God ask of you but to fear the LORD your God, to walk in his ways, to love him, to serve the LORD your God with all your heart and with all your soul.

Deuteronomy 10:12

My Relationships As a Christian Woman
How to Guide in Problem Situations

But now you must rid yourselves of all such things as these: anger, rage, malice, slander, filthy language.

Colossians 3:8

August 11

My Relationships As a Christian Woman
How to Enrich My Relationships

I care very little if I am judged by you, or by any human court; indeed, I do not even judge myself. My conscience is clear, but that does not make me innocent. It is the Lord who judges me. Therefore judge nothing before the appointed time; wait till the Lord comes. He will bring to light what is hidden in darkness and will expose the motives of men's hearts. At that time each will receive his praise from God.

1 Corinthians 4:3–5

May 23

My Relationships As a Christian Woman
How to Guide in Problem Situations

He who answers before listening—that is his folly and his shame.
Proverbs 18:13

August 10

My Relationships As a Christian Woman
How to Enrich My Relationships

If you lend money to one of my people among you who is needy, do not be like a moneylender; charge him no interest.

Exodus 22:25

May 24

My Relationships As a Christian Woman
How to Recognize a Good Church

Every day they continued to meet together in the temple courts. They broke bread in their homes and ate together with glad and sincere hearts, praising God and enjoying the favor of all the people. And the Lord added to their number daily those who were being saved.

Acts 2:46–47

August 9

My Relationships As a Christian Woman
How to Relate to Leaders

Young men, in the same way be submissive to those who are older. Clothe yourselves with humility toward one another, because, "God opposes the proud but gives grace to the humble." Humble yourselves, therefore, under God's mighty hand, that he may lift you up in due time.

1 Peter 5:5–6

My Relationships As a Christian Woman
My Role in the Body of Christ

*A*lways give yourselves fully to the work of the LORD, because you know that your labor in the Lord is not in vain.

I Corinthians 15:58

August 8

My Relationships As a Christian Woman
How to Be a Leader

I myself will tend my sheep and have them lie down, declares the Sovereign LORD. I will search for the lost and bring back the strays. I will bind up the injured and strengthen the weak.

Ezekiel 34:15–16

May 26

My Relationships As a Christian Woman
My Spiritual Gifts

Even on my servants, both men and women, I will pour out my Spirit in those days.
Acts 2:18

August 7

My Relationships As a Christian Woman
My Attitudes Toward Others

You must not associate with anyone who calls himself a brother but is sexually immoral or greedy, an idolater or a slanderer, a drunkard or a swindler. With such a man do not even eat. God will judge those outside. "Expel the wicked man from among you."

1 Corinthians 5:11,13

My Inner Life As a Christian Woman
How I Get the Most From Scripture

This is what the LORD says: "Stand at the crossroads and look; ask for the ancient paths, ask where the good way is, and walk in it, and you will find rest for your souls."

Jeremiah 6:16

August 6

My Relationships As a Christian Woman
My Giving

Remember this: whoever sows sparingly will also reap sparingly, and whoever sows generously will also reap generously.

2 Corinthians 9:6

May 28

My Inner Life As a Christian Woman
How I Develop a Prayer Life

And whatever you do, whether in word or deed, do it all in the name of the Lord Jesus, giving thanks to God the Father through him.

Colossians 3:17

My Identity As a Christian Woman

I Am Destined for Eternal Glory

I the LORD search the heart and examine the mind, to reward a man according to his conduct, according to what his deeds deserve.

Jeremiah 17:10

My Inner Life As a Christian Woman
How I Develop a Praise Life

O LORD, you are my God; I will exalt you and praise your name, for in perfect faithfulness you have done marvelous things, things planned long ago.

Isaiah 25:1

August 4

My Identity As a Christian Woman
I Am Growing More Christlike

We . . . are being transformed into his likeness with ever-increasing glory, which comes from the Lord, who is the Spirit.

2 Corinthians 3:18

My Inner Life As a Christian Woman
How I Overcome Temptations

Consider it pure joy, my brothers, whenever you face trials of many kinds, because you know that the testing of your faith develops perseverance. Perseverance must finish its work so that you may be mature and complete, not lacking anything.

James 1:2–4

August 3

My Identity As a Christian Woman
I Am Guarded by God's Power

Be strong and courageous. Do not be afraid or terrified because of them, for the LORD your God goes with you; he will never leave you nor forsake you.

Deuteronomy 31:6

My Inner Life As a Christian Woman

How I Deal With Pride

Who can discern his errors? Forgive my hidden faults.

Psalm 19:12

August 2

My Identity As a Christian Woman
I Am Guided Through Life

Teach me your way, O LORD, and I will walk in your truth; give me an undivided heart, that I may fear your name. I will praise you, O LORD my God, with all my heart; I will glorify your name forever.

Psalm 86:11–12

June 1

My Identity As a Christian Woman
I Am Called to Be a Disciple

Looking at his disciples, he [Jesus] said: "Blessed are you who are poor, for yours is the kingdom of God. Blessed are you who hunger now, for you will be satisfied. Blessed are you who weep now, for you will laugh. Blessed are you when men hate you, when they exclude you and insult you and reject your name as evil, because of the Son of Man."

Luke 6:20–22

August 1

My Identity As a Christian Woman
I Am Called to Be a Disciple

The LORD your God is with you, he is mighty to save. He will take great delight in you, he will quiet you with his love, he will rejoice over you with singing.

Zephaniah 3:17

My Identity As a Christian Woman
I Am Guided Through Life

Teach me to do your will, for you are my God; may your good Spirit lead me on level ground.

Psalms 143:10

July 31

My Inner Life As a Christian Woman
How I Deal With Pride

This is what the LORD says: "Cursed is the one who trusts in man, who depends on flesh for his strength and whose heart turns away from the LORD." But blessed is the man who trusts in the LORD, whose confidence is in him.

Jeremiah 17:5,7

My Identity As a Christian Woman
I Am Guarded by God's Power

He is able to keep you from falling and to present you before his glorious presence without fault and with great joy.

Jude 24

July 30

My Inner Life As a Christian Woman

How I Overcome Temptations

Yet this is what the Sovereign LORD says: "It will not take place, it will not happen. If you do not stand firm in your faith, you will not stand at all."

Isaiah 7:7,9

June 4

My Identity As a Christian Woman
I Am Growing More Christlike

Dear friends, now we are children of God, and what we will be has not yet been made known. But we know that when he appears, we shall be like him, for we shall see him as he is. Everyone who has this hope in him purifies himself, just as he is pure.

1 John 3:2–3

July 29

My Inner Life As a Christian Woman

How I Develop a Praise Life

But I trust in your unfailing love; my heart rejoices in your salvation. I will sing to the LORD, for he has been good to me.

Psalm 13:5–6

My Identity As a Christian Woman
I Am Destined for Eternal Glory

When the perishable has been clothed with the imperishable, and the mortal with immortality, then the saying that is written will come true: "Death has been swallowed up in victory."

1 Corinthians 15:54

My Inner Life As a Christian Woman

How I Develop a Prayer Life

*G*ive thanks to the LORD, for he is good; his love endures forever.
Psalm 107:1

June 6

My Relationships As a Christian Woman
My Fellowship With Others

But if we walk in the light, as he is in the light, we have fellowship with one another, and the blood of Jesus, his Son, purifies us from all sin.

1 John 1:7

July 27

My Inner Life As a Christian Woman
How I Get the Most From Scripture

But the man who looks intently into the perfect law that gives freedom, and continues to do this, not forgetting what he has heard, but doing it—he will be blessed in what he does.

James 1:25

June 7

My Relationships As a Christian Woman
My Giving

Our desire is not that others might be relieved while you are hard pressed, but that there might be an equality. At the present time your plenty will supply what they need, so that in turn their plenty will supply what you need. Then there will be equality.

2 Corinthians 8:13–14

July 26

My Relationships As a Christian Woman
My Fellowship With Others

If it is possible, as far as it depends on you, live at peace with everyone.
Romans 12:18

June 8

My Relationships As a Christian Woman
My Attitudes Toward Others

Accept him whose faith is weak, without passing judgment on disputable matters.
Romans 14:1

July 25

My Relationships As a Christian Woman
My Spiritual Gifts

Each one should use whatever gift he has received to serve others, faithfully administering God's grace in its various forms. If anyone speaks, he should do it as one speaking the very words of God. If anyone serves, he should do it with the strength God provides, so that in all things God may be praised through Jesus Christ.

1 Peter 4:10–11

June 9

My Relationships As a Christian Woman
How to Be a Leader

*L*eaders must be worthy of respect, sincere, not indulging in much wine, and not pursuing dishonest gain. They must keep hold of the deep truths of the faith with a clear conscience. They must first be tested and then if there is nothing against them, let them serve.

1 Timothy 3:8–10

July 24

My Relationships As a Christian Woman
My Role in the Body of Christ

Set an example for the believers in speech, in life, in love, in faith and in purity.
1 Timothy 4:12

June 10

My Relationships As a Christian Woman
How to Relate to Leaders

Remember your leaders, who spoke the word of God to you. Consider the outcome of their way of life and imitate their faith.

Hebrews 13:7

July 23

My Relationships As a Christian Woman
How to Recognize a Good Church

Do not be carried away by all kinds of strange teachings. It is good for our hearts to be strengthened by grace, not by ceremonial foods, which are of no value to those who eat them.

Hebrews 13:9

June 11

My Relationships As a Christian Woman
How to Enrich My Relationships

Pray in the Spirit on all occasions with all kinds of prayer and requests. With this in mind, be alert and always keep on praying for all the saints.

Ephesians 6:18

July 22

My Relationships As a Christian Woman
How to Guide in Problem Situations

He who conceals his sin does not prosper, but whoever confesses and renounces them finds mercy.

Proverbs 28:13

June 12

My Relationships As a Christian Woman

How to Enrich My Relationships

Each of us should please his neighbor for his good, to build him up.
Romans 15:2

July 21

My Relationships As a Christian Woman
How to Guide in Problem Situations

Do not follow the crowd in doing wrong.

Exodus 23:2

My Relationships As a Christian Woman
How Christian Values Differ

What is highly valued among men is detestable in God's sight.
                                                    Luke 16:15

July 20

My Relationships As a Christian Woman
How to Tell My Child About God

Teach and admonish one another with all wisdom, and as you sing psalms, hymns and spiritual songs with gratitude in your hearts to God. And whatever you do, whether in word or deed, do it all in the name of the Lord Jesus, giving thanks to God the Father through him.

Colossians 3:16–17

June 14

My Relationships As a Christian Woman
My Attitude Toward the World

Do not store up for yourselves treasures on earth, where moth and rust destroy, and where thieves break in and steal. But store up for yourselves treasures in heaven, where moth and rust do not destroy, and where thieves do not break in and steal. For where your treasure is, there your heart will be also.

Matthew 6:19–21

July 19

My Relationships As a Christian Woman

How to Communicate Love

I will not take my love from him, nor will I ever betray my faithfulness.
Psalm 89:33

June 15

My Relationships As a Christian Woman
My Attitude Toward Non-Christians

Hear me, you who know what is right, you people who have my law in your hearts: Do not fear the reproach of men or be terrified by their insults.

Isaiah 51:7

July 18

My Relationships As a Christian Woman
How to Pray for My Children

And I pray that you, being rooted and established in love, may have power, together with all the saints, to grasp how wide and long and high and deep is the love of Christ, and to know this love that surpasses knowledge—that you may be filled to the measure of all the fullness of God.

Ephesians 3:17–19

My Relationships As a Christian Woman
My Relationships With Non-Christians

But even if you should suffer for what is right, you are blessed. "Do not fear what they fear; do not be frightened." But in your hearts set apart Christ as Lord. Always be prepared to give an answer to everyone who asks you to give the reason for the hope that you have. But do this with gentleness and respect.

1 Peter 3:14–15

July 17

My Relationships As a Christian Woman
How to Encourage Spiritual Growth

The secret things belong to the LORD our God, but the things revealed belong to us and to our children forever, that we may follow all the words of this law.

Deuteronomy 29:29

June 17

My Relationships As a Christian Woman
My Attitude Toward Materialism

But godliness with contentment is great gain. For we brought nothing into the world, and we can take nothing out of it. But if we have food and clothing, we will be content with that.

1 Timothy 6:6–8

July 16

My Relationships As a Christian Woman
My Resources for Discipline

The rod of correction imparts wisdom, but a child left to itself disgraces his mother.
Proverbs 29:15

June 18

My Relationships As a Christian Woman
My Responsibilities as a Citizen

Do you want to be free from the fear of the one in authority? Then do what is right and he will commend you. For he is God's servant to do you good. But if you do wrong, be afraid, for he does not bear the sword for nothing. . . . Therefore, it is necessary to submit to the authorities, not only because of possible punishment but also because of conscience.

Romans 13:3–5

July 15

My Relationships As a Christian Woman
My Purpose in Discipline

He will die for lack of discipline, led astray by his own great folly.
Proverbs 5:23

My Relationships As a Christian Woman
My Responsibilities to the Poor

*I*s this not the kind of fasting I have chosen: to loose the chains of injustice and untie the cords of the yoke, to set the oppressed free and break every yoke?

Isaiah 58:6–8

July 14

My Relationships As a Christian Woman
My Goals in Child Rearing

As dearly loved children . . . live a life of love, just as Christ loved us and gave himself up for us as a fragrant offering and sacrifice to God.

Ephesians 5:1–2

My Relationships As a Christian Woman
My Responsibilities to Individuals

He has showed you, O man, what is good. And what does the LORD require of you? To act justly and to love mercy and to walk humbly with your God.

Micah 6:8

July 13

My Relationships As a Christian Woman
How to Mother

In everything set them an example by doing what is good. In your teaching show integrity, seriousness.

Titus 2:7

My Relationships As a Christian Woman
How to Introduce a Person to Jesus

For God so loved the world that he gave his one and only Son, that whoever believes in him shall not perish but have eternal life.

John 3:16

July 12

My Relationships As a Christian Woman
My Attitude Toward Forgiveness

Be kind and compassionate to one another, forgiving each other, just as in Christ God forgave you.

Ephesians 4:32

June 22

My Relationships As a Christian Woman
My Attitude Toward Money

No one can serve two masters. Either he will hate the one and love the other, or he will be devoted to the one and despise the other. You cannot serve both God and Money.

Matthew 6:24

July 11

My Relationships As a Christian Woman
My Attitude Toward Openness

We, who with unveiled faces all reflect the Lord's glory, are being transformed into his likeness with ever-increasing glory, which comes from the Lord, who is the Spirit.
2 Corinthians 3:18

June 23

My Relationships As a Christian Woman

My Attitude Toward Work

In the name of the Lord Jesus Christ, we command you, brothers, to keep away from every brother who is idle and does not live according to the teaching you received from us. For you yourselves know how you ought to follow our example. We were not idle when we were with you, nor did we eat anyone's food without paying for it. On the contrary, we worked night and day, laboring and toiling so that we would not be a burden to any of you. We did this, not because we do not have the right to such help, but in order to make ourselves a model for you to follow. For even when we were with you, we gave you this rule: "If a man will not work, he shall not eat."

2 Thessalonians 3:6–10

July 10

My Relationships As a Christian Woman
My Approach to Weakness

Encourage one another and build each other up, just as in fact you are doing.
1 Thessalonians 5:11

June 24

My Relationships As a Christian Woman
God's Ideal for My Marriage

Therefore, as God's chosen people, holy and dearly loved, clothe yourselves with compassion, kindness, humility, gentleness and patience. Bear with each other and forgive whatever grievances you may have against one another. Forgive as the Lord forgave you. And over all these virtues put on love, which binds them all together in perfect unity. Let the peace of Christ rule in your hearts, since as members of one body you were called to peace. And be thankful.

Colossians 3:12–15

July 9

My Relationships As a Christian Woman
My Approach to Anger

The fruit of righteousness will be peace; the effect of righteousness will be quietness and confidence forever.

Isaiah 32:17

June 25

My Relationships As a Christian Woman
My Role As a Wife

Submit to one another out of reverence for Christ.

Ephesians 5:21

July 8

My Relationships As a Christian Woman

My Approach to Hurt

Give, and it will be given to you. A good measure, pressed down, shaken together and running over, will be poured into your lap. For with the measure you use, it will be measured to you.

Luke 6:38

June 26

My Inner Life As a Christian Woman

How I Overcome Temptations

When tempted, no one should say, "God is tempting me." For God cannot be tempted by evil, nor does he tempt anyone; but each one is tempted when, by his own evil desire, he is dragged away and enticed.

James 1:13–14

July 7

My Relationships As a Christian Woman

My Approach to Conflict

He who ignores discipline comes to poverty and shame, but whoever heeds correction is honored.

Proverbs 13:18

June 27

My Inner Life As a Christian Woman
How I Deal With Loneliness

Serve one another in love.

Galatians 5:13

July 6

My Relationships As a Christian Woman

My Attitude Toward Sex

The wife's body does not belong to her alone but also to her husband. In the same way, the husband's body does not belong to him alone but to the wife. Do not deprive each other.

1 Corinthians 7:4–5

June 28

My Inner Life As a Christian Woman
How I Deal With Discouragement

I pray also that the eyes of your heart may be enlightened in order that you may know the hope to which he has called you, the riches of his glorious inheritance in the saints, and his incomparably great power for us who believe.

Ephesians 1:18–19

July 5

My Identity As a Christian Woman
I Am Gifted to Serve Others

*I*n the last days, God says, I will pour out my Spirit on all people. Your sons and daughters will prophesy, your young men will see visions, your old men will dream dreams. Even on my servants, both men and women, I will pour out my Spirit in those days, and they will prophesy.

Acts 2:17–18

June 29

My Inner Life As a Christian Woman
How I Channel My Thought Life

Let the wicked forsake his way and the evil man his thoughts. Let him turn to the LORD, and he will have mercy on him, and to our God, for he will freely pardon.

Isaiah 55:7

July 4

My Identity As a Christian Woman

I Am Indwelt by God's Spirit

If the Spirit of him who raised Jesus from the dead is living in you, he who raised Christ from the dead will also give life to your mortal bodies through his Spirit, who lives in you.

Romans 8:11

Independence Day

My Inner Life As a Christian Woman
How I Deal With Anxiety and Worry

Who of you by worrying can add a single hour to his life? Since you cannot do this very little thing, why do you worry about the rest?

Luke 12:25–26

July 3

My Identity As a Christian Woman
I Am Part of God's Family

Be imitators of God, therefore, as dearly loved children and live a life of love, just as Christ loved us and gave himself up for us as a fragrant offering and sacrifice to God.

Ephesians 5:1–2

July 1

My Identity As a Christian Woman
I Am Created in God's Image

Your hands made me and formed me; give me understanding to learn your commands. May they who fear you rejoice when they see me, for I have put my hope in your word.

Psalm 119:73–74

July 2

My Identity As a Christian Woman
I Am Saved by Christ's Sacrifice

For God so loved the world that he gave his one and only Son, that whoever believes in him shall not perish but have eternal life.

John 3:16